THE
SQUIRREL
AND THE
LOST
TREASURE

for
Mum

PARTICULAR BOOKS
MMXXIII

Vauxhall, London
SW1V 2SA

Also by this author
The Fox and the Star
The Worm and the Bird
The Song of the Tree

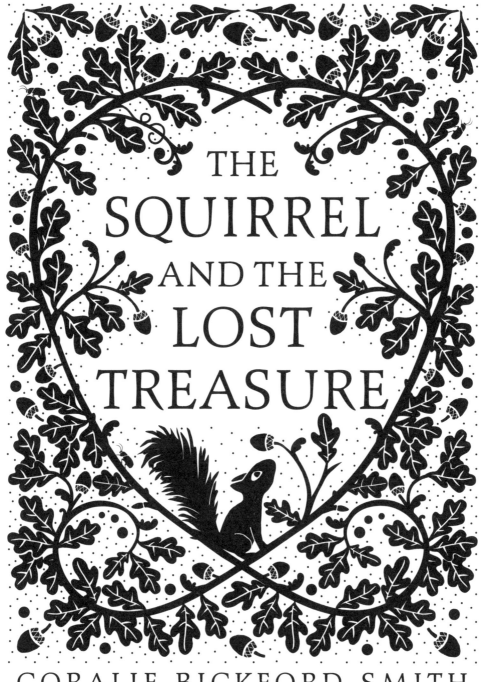

THE
SQUIRREL
AND THE
LOST
TREASURE

CORALIE BICKFORD-SMITH

As the sun
set over an
ancient forest,
a young squirrel
watched the
shadows grow.

Autumn leaves
surrendered
to the wind
and acorns fell
to the ground …

... soon to be
snatched up
by busy paws.

Rustling,
snuffling,
nibbling.

Squirrel looked on curiously, listening to the murmurs below.

They spoke of a place in the heart of the forest where no trees grow.

As dusk settled, the sky was etched with starlight.

A sense
of calm
drifted
through the
branches.

Squirrel saw
a solitary
acorn
glinting
on the
forest floor.

She
dropped
down,
crunching
the
leaves
at
her
feet.

Clutching her
shiny treasure,
she drifted
off to sleep,
determined
never to let go.

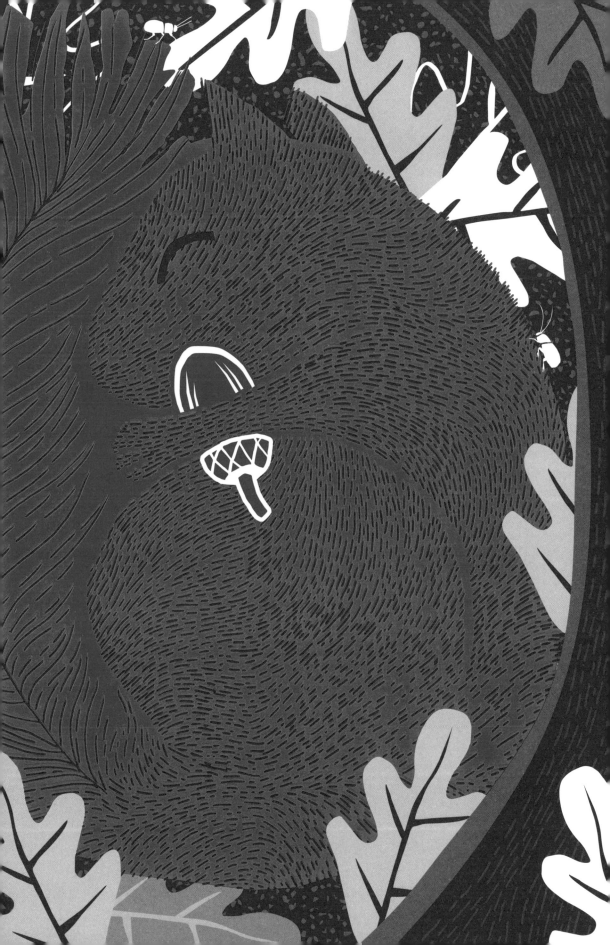

As dawn
broke,
Squirrel
rose with
a start.

'I must hide
my acorn far
away from
watchful eyes
and hungry
mouths.'

She scuttled

towards the

shadows,

deeper into

the heart

of the

forest ...

...to a place
with no trees,
no birdsong
and no squirrels.

A perfect space
where her acorn
might be safe.

The silence
made her
shiver.

She buried her
acorn deep
in the earth –
hidden from view
and safe from
the cold.

Winter

came

with icy

winds.

It

seemed

to last

forever.

Squirrel
foraged for
food by day,
longing for
the heat of
the sun.

At night,
tucked deep
inside her tree,
she dreamed
of her buried
treasure.

Until one day
the sun's rays
grew warmer.
Buds of green
sprouted from
branches,
and the forest
began to stir.

Missing
her acorn,
Squirrel
set off . . .

... back to the
place where
no trees grow.

She was sure
of the spot and
began to dig.

But her
acorn was no
longer there.

Where
could
it be?

Summer
came
and
went.

Soon the
forest was
changing
again . . .

... Squirrel was
changing too.

This time she
joined the others,
racing to collect
the fallen treasure.

Rustling,
snuffling,
nibbling.

Back and forth,
she scurried
to the heart
of the forest,
burying all
the acorns she
could find –
deep in the earth,
safe from the cold.

Hopeful

that

just

one

would

remain.

Winter

came

once

more.

It

seemed

to last

forever.

At the first
signs of spring,
Squirrel rushed
to the heart
of the forest.

She looked
everywhere.

Her acorns
were nowhere
to be found.

'Where could they have gone?' she cried.

As the
shadows
grew longer,
Squirrel lost
all hope.

Slowly
she
returned
home.

Squirrel woke
up to the
sound of
hungry chicks
and rustling
leaves.

New life
was all
around
her.

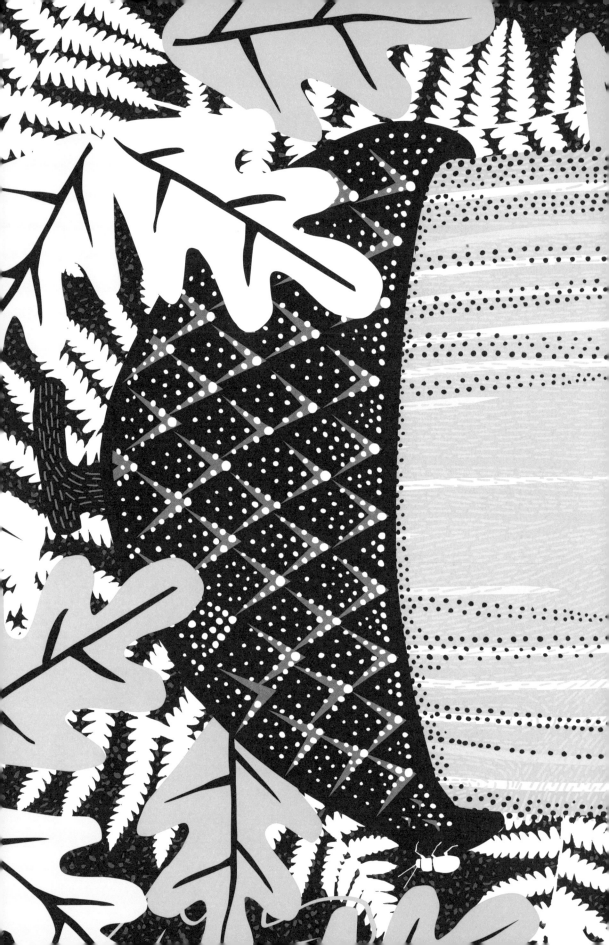

She began
to wonder ...

'If life
is always
changing ...

could an acorn

change too?'

Squirrel
hurried back.

This time
she just
looked ...

'Yes,

they do.

Acorns

change

too!'

And with each
passing year
Squirrel's
treasure grew,
filling the heart
of the forest.

Thank you
Natalia O'Hara, David Mackintosh,
Tom Lehman and Jim Stoddart

PARTICULAR BOOKS

UK | USA | Canada | Ireland | Australia
India | New Zealand | South Africa

Particular Books is part of the Penguin Random House group of companies
whose addresses can be found at global.penguinrandomhouse.com.

First published 2023
001

Set in Wile 12/15pt by Coralie Bickford-Smith
Printed in Italy by L.E.G.O. S.p.A. on Munken Pure Rough

The authorized representative in the EEA is Penguin Random House Ireland,
Morrison Chambers, 32 Nassau Street, Dublin D02 YH68

A CIP catalogue record for this book is available from the British Library

ISBN: 978–0–241–54197–5

Penguin Random House is committed to a sustainable
future for our business, our readers and our planet.
This book is made from Forest Stewardship Council® certified paper.

www.greenpenguin.co.uk

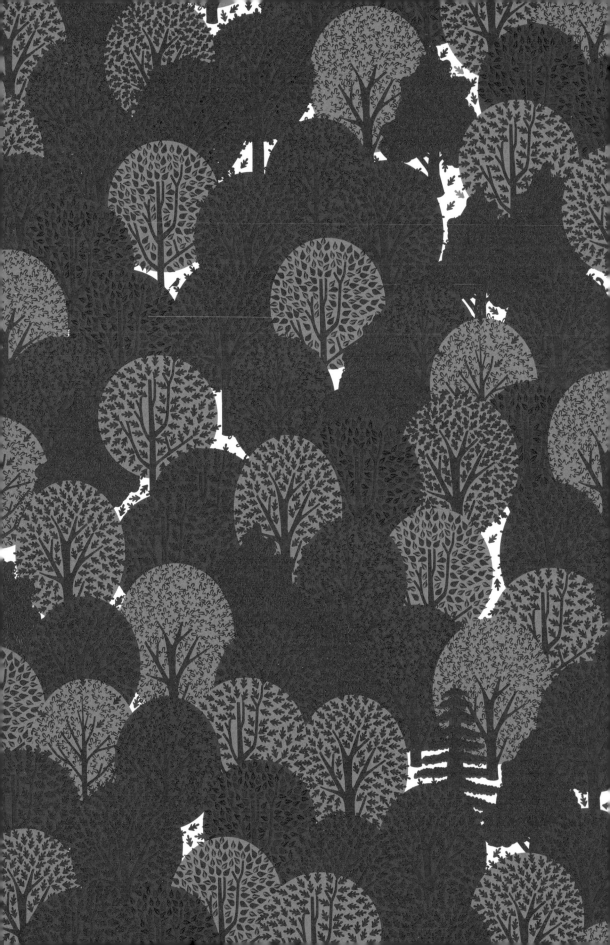